⟶ **52** ⟵
WAYS TO
BE A GREAT
MOTHER-
IN-LAW

Other Books by the Author

The Marriage Track

Beating the Winter Blues

Sanity in the Summertime

60 One-Minute Marriage Builders

60 One-Minute Family Builders

60 One-Minute Memory Makers

52 Dates for You and Your Mate

52
WAYS TO
BE A GREAT
MOTHER-
IN-LAW

Claudia Arp

Thomas Nelson Publishers
Nashville

3460

All of the characters in the stories are composites of the hundreds of people the Arps have met and talked with during the years of their work in family enrichment. Names, genders, and other identifying characteristics have been changed to protect the privacy of those people.

Published in Nashville, Tennessee, by Janet Thoma Books, a division of Thomas Nelson, Inc., Publishers, and distributed in Canada by Word Communications, Ltd., Richmond, British Columbia, and in the United Kingdom by Word (UK), Ltd., Milton Keynes, England.

Library of Congress Cataloging-in-Publication Data

Arp, Claudia.
    52 ways to be a great mother-in-law / by Claudia Arp.
      p.   cm.
    ISBN 0-8407-6897-4
    1. Mothers-in-law. I. Title.   II. Title: Fifty-two ways to be a great mother-in-law.
HQ759.25.A78   1993
647.7′8—dc20   93-9863
                                              CIP

Printed in the United States of America

1 2 3 4 5 6 — 98 97 96 95 94 93

Acknowledgements

I am grateful to the mothers-in-law and daughters- and sons-in-law who shared their experiences and advice with me. I especially want to thank Jane Bell for her help and encouragement, and my own mother-in-law and daughters-in-law who continue to enrich my life.

Special thanks to the in-house staff of Thomas Nelson and to my favorite editors at Janet Thoma Books—Susan, Laurie, Janet, you're the best!

Contents

To Lillian

The Secret of Being a Great Mother-in-Law

Why all the jokes about mothers-in-law? Why don't we laugh about fathers-in-law? Actually, mother-in-law jokes are no laughing matter. Research confirms that the most difficult in-law relationship is that of mother-in-law and daughter-in-law. Since we had only boys, this bit of information was not encouraging to me.

As our sons began to marry, I really wanted to be a great mother-in-law, but frankly, I didn't know how. So I began to talk to those who had more experience than I did. I also talked with many young daughters-in-law. I soon discovered that in most in-law relationships, the mother-in-law is the key player. Scary as it was, I discovered that there were some things I could do to build positive in-law relationships. I discovered that in-laws don't have to be outlaws. And I began to get excited that, at last, I wasn't the only female in our family! Things were looking up!

The Positives of Being a Mother-in-Law

Think about all the positive aspects of being a mother-in-law. For instance, picture having:

- A daughter you never have to argue with about make-up and weird clothes.
- A son you don't have to "pray home" in the wee hours of the morning or cart to 10,000 soccer games.
- An adult son or daughter without a history of parental hassles.
- An opportunity to have an adult relationship with someone with whom you have at least one major thing in common—a love of your son or daughter.

It can really happen. Listen to what some mothers-in-law have to say:

- "I get to enjoy my grandchildren, and I just love it that my son and daughter-in-law actually want to come to visit me!"
- "I've lived through the parenting years, now I'm enjoying the pleasure years."
- "It's great to simply enjoy this relationship and not feel responsible!"
- "I love not having to compete or control anything."
- "This is the best stage of family life yet!"

My Own Experience

I was a great mom before I had kids. I was a great mother-in-law before I had married kids. I decided I'd be just like my mother-in-law, Lillian. She made it so easy to love her. She never interfered, I always felt accepted—it looked so easy!

I've been a daughter-in-law for more than thirty years, a mother-in-law for almost five. I'm definitely in the learning stages, but being a great mother-in-law like Lillian is not easy. Having wonderful daughters-in-law helps, but I must confess, I'm still learning. And I'm the number one benefactor of this book.

What Lillian Did Right

I don't know how hard it was for Lillian to love me. I only know she always has. If I've learned anything as a daughter-in-law over the last thirty years, Lillian has been my teacher, and it is to this very special lady that I dedicate this book. Lillian, thanks for your role model and for all the years you spent building into Dave the many things I love and admire in him.

Recently I asked my mother-in-law how she did it, and she replied, "Well, I didn't do anything." Was her modesty showing? Or is there a great principle here —when in doubt, do nothing!

I also want to thank my daughters-in-law for their encouragement and the permission to compile this book. They make it easy for me to love and respect them. My sons are very fortunate indeed.

What's the Secret?

After talking to hundreds of mothers-in-law and daughters- and sons-in-law, I've compiled their sage advice. The good news is that even if your relationship as a mother-in-law is at present shaky, you can make a change. Take a tip each week on relating positively to your in-laws, and you can see your relationships become healthy and happy ones.

Aim for a Change of Attitude and Action

In the following chapter you will find 52 practical things I learned from Lillian and other seasoned mothers-in-law. Unlike books that are for passive reading, this book is for active participation.

Relationships are fluid and ever changing. Hopefully the following suggestions will help your in-law relationships change for the better. Change can begin in several ways. It can begin with a new idea, so each chapter focuses on one central idea as a goal to aim toward.

Change can also begin with a change in attitude. So each idea is stated in the form of an attitude to work into your in-law relationship. Change can also occur through action, so each chapter concludes with practical things that you can do.

Have fun with this book. Here are 52 ways to be a great mother-in-law, 52 things to aim for, to challenge you to change your attitude, to act out each day in your relationship with that special son- or daughter-in-law. The rest is up to you.

1 ❀ "Stand Beside Not Between"

"As parents we promise to stand beside not between." That's a line from the liturgy of one of our sons' weddings—the line that is most prominent in my memory. It gives a beautiful picture of how I am to relate to my sons and daughters-in-law. Remembering it, however, is one thing, actually doing it is another! Easy or not, it's the key to being a great mother in law!

Consider my mother-in-law, Lillian. I remember vividly the first time Lillian stood beside me. I had yet to meet her but was engaged to her only son. Lillian was living in Naples, Italy, when Dave and I decided to get married at Christmas in Ellijay, Georgia. It wasn't an easy time of the year to get a military family from Naples to the mountains of North Georgia. But Lillian's determination resulted in Dave's family's presence at our wedding.

I actually met Lillian in the Atlanta airport three days before the wedding. I discovered right away that she had purposely left her advice in Italy. From the beginning Lillian stood beside us in a loving, supportive, and noncontrolling way.

Attitude: **I want to let go while remaining supportive.**

Letting go is being willing to take a lower priority in your son's or daughter's life. Your part is to play second fiddle, and that is OK. A key problem in marriages, not only in America but all over the world, is the failure of mothers to let go of their children. This may be particularly difficult if you are very close to your child. It's not easy to stand beside and encourage your child to make it his or her first priority to please his or her spouse rather than mom and dad. In many cultures and economic situations, families live with parents and grandparents. While I don't recommend this kind of living relationship, the key is letting go emotionally, which goes much deeper than physically distancing yourself.

Action: **Ways to stand beside**

- Give a special gift to your future in-law.
- Realize that the wedding is theirs. One friend told me, "I'm getting along great with my future daughter-in-law. She's in a continual battle for control with her mom. I simply give no opinion, so I'm the good guy!"
- Don't interfere. Whatever they choose to do, when the ceremony is over, they will be married and you will be a mother-in-law.

2 ❋ Give Unconditional Acceptance

I knew it was a mistake when I had my "colors" done. Frosted hair and my natural coloring just don't go together! Now that my hair is naturally frosted, I cover it up, but for a couple of years when we were first married I went through the frosted hair stage. Other people in my life wasted no time telling me how bad I looked, but not Lillian.

It's sad to say, but relationships can be wrecked over something as superficial as hairstyle or the way someone dresses. I know one person who actually changed her attitude toward her daughter-in-law because she cut her hair too short. Another in-law relationship I know was totally shipwrecked because the daughter-in-law's kitchen wasn't clean enough to eat off the floor. Lillian may have been tempted at times to critique me in many ways, but she said not a word.

Attitude: *I accept my daughter- or son-in-law, period.*

Realize that your self-worth is not based on what your daughter- or son-in-law does or doesn't do. He or she is not a reflection of your family—that is, unless it's a positive reflection!

Ask yourself, "What is more important—the relationship with my son- or daughter-in-law or what my friends think?" This question may help when you're about to react to something that isn't worth damaging the relationship over. (On the other hand, do you embarrass your son- or daughter-in-law? It goes both ways!)

Action: Ways to show acceptance

- Never criticize the way your son-in-law dresses or your daughter-in-law wears her make-up. One mother-in-law put it this way, "Only look at their eyes. That's all that counts."
- Watch your nonverbal communication! It's easy to criticize without saying a word. We all know "the look."
- Remember, whatever you would like to change is probably temporary. Those people who didn't like my frosted hair now wish I would let the gray show naturally.

3 • Resist the Urge to Give Advice

I knew I should have been quiet. But in today's world where divorce is epidemic, the uncontrolled words just popped out of my mouth. "Please, don't ever kid about divorce!"

Their nonverbal reaction told me I had overstepped my boundaries. And I once again realized that there are much better ways to build the relationships with my daughters-in-law than giving unrequested advice.

I learned to zip my lip. And when I do slip, I've learned to apologize. Even one year later, it isn't too late to say you're sorry. That's how long it took me to apologize for giving my "don't kid about divorce" advice. Even at that late date, I was forgiven.

Attitude: I will acknowledge that giving advice will not build our relationship.

The one thing I desire the most with my daughters-in-law is to have a healthy, open relationship with each of them. When I actively think about the positives, like the ways they complement my sons and the wonderful unique treasures they bring to our growing extended family, I am less inclined to be critical and to give advice. Often I ask myself, "Is what I'm about to say going to build trust or tear down trust in the relationship?"

Action: Ways to resist giving advice

- Bite your tongue if you have to. Remember it is in a slippery place!
- Give a compliment instead of a critique.
- When asked for advice, weigh carefully what you say. Substitute an ounce of advice for each pound you'd like to give. And end with this sentence: "I'm sure you'll make the best decision."
- Follow this general principle—if in doubt, don't!

4 ❋ Include Your In-Law in Family Memories

When an Arp son shows a young lady our Family Slide Show, we take notice! To this point, two sons have presented it, and we have two daughters-in-law. Family memories are for sharing, and they help the new family members (or family members to be) feel included.

A couple of years ago while visiting Dave's parents, we pulled out all the old boxes of pictures, newspaper clippings, and family history. We had a ball looking through all the Arp history. I loved all the cute pictures of Dave as a little boy, but what really fascinated me were the pictures and articles about Lillian.

I could visualize her as the young mother of two little children and could almost feel her love and devotion to her family. Being a military family, they lived all over the world. I imagined how she provided the stability and emotional comfort for her family's many transitions. It gave me a new appreciation and love for this lady who so influenced the one person I love more than anyone else in the whole world.

Attitude: *I want my son- or daughter-in-law to feel included.*

No one wants to be on the outside looking in, but it's easy for an in-law to feel that way. Today cross-cultural marriages are common. Being bilingual can present its own unique challenge.

The first time my friend Helga's daughter-in-law visited them, Helga and her husband from time to time lapsed into German. It wasn't smart on their part. Their daughter-in-law had enough things to adjust to in a cross-cultural marriage—she didn't need a language barrier as well.

I must admit, we've been guilty of speaking German around our daughters-in-law. We lived in Austria when our boys were growing up, and one benefit was learning a second language. When the boys were young they used German to ask us questions they didn't want anyone else to hear. But when in-laws are around this is not kind, and we stopped doing it.

Basically it's a question of attitude. Do you really want your in-laws to feel a part of your family? Then look for ways to include them!

Action: *Ways to make your in-laws feel included*

- Intentionally include them in your conversations.
- Share old pictures, newspaper clippings, videos, slides, or whatever family memories you have.
- Take lots of pictures that include them.

- Take a trip together.
- Show genuine interest in their family traditions.
- Be willing to learn something new from them.

5 ❖ Process Your History with Your Own Mother and Mother-in-Law

If your relationship with your son or daughter-in-law mirrored your relationship with the mothers in your life, would it be positive or negative? What kind of daughter and daughter-in-law have you been? Those relationships have a direct bearing on how you relate to your own daughter- or son-in-law.

Consider your relationship with your own mother and mother-in-law. Are there issues that need resolving? If so, we often slip back into looking to others for affirmation and approval as if we were still children. When others push our buttons, we react.

For instance, Martha, at age fifty-two, is still controlled by her mother. She checks in daily with her mother, and if she misses a day, her mother lets her know about it. Major holidays are a command performance. As a mother-in-law she tends to be distant—she doesn't want to be too possessive and repeat history.

Then there is Nora. The family she grew up in is basically out of touch with each other. She tries to give her daughter and son-in-law the attention she didn't get from her own mother and can best be described as a hovering helicopter. Both Martha and

Nora need to adjust their perspective and have an attitude check.

Attitude: Healthy mother or mother-in-law relationships can begin with me.

Past mother relationships affect present in-law relationships. We tend to repeat our parent's mistakes or go to the other extreme. If you hate being manipulated emotionally, watch out—you may be a candidate for a repeat performance! You may need to go beyond the examples of the mothers in your life and choose different role models whom you want to follow.

You are an adult. With adult status comes the responsibility for your own decisions. You are not responsible for your mother's or your mother-in-law's decisions or happiness. Remember you are not responsible for what you can't control. But change can begin today, and it can begin with you.

Think about what you can do today to improve the relationship with the mothers in your life. Do you need to forgive or ask for forgiveness? Are you willing to choose to love?

Action: Ways to process your past

- Take the initiative to apologize and to forgive your mother or mother-in-law if needed.
- Call your own mother or mother-in-law just to say hello—have no agenda and keep the phone call short.
- Write a letter to your mother or mother-in-law

and mention those things you appreciate about her.

- Never use manipulation as a weapon with either generation.
- Empathize with your mother-in-law, but don't assume responsibility for her happiness.

6 ❄ Find Things That Make Your Daughter- or Son-in-Law Feel Comfortable

For years whenever we visited Dave's parents, I could always count on finding corn candy on a certain shelf in the kitchen. That's one thing Lillian and I have in common—our "sweet tooth"—and we both liked corn candy. The corn candy was a simple act of thoughtfulness but one I still remember years later. Now we're into chocolate-covered Oreo cookies.

Think about your own son- or daughter-in-law. Do you know one or two things that make him or her feel comfortable?

Attitude: I will look for little likes and dislikes, for small ways to be hospitable to my son- or daughter-in-law.

Observe your son- or daughter-in-law and look for little ways to add to his or her comfort. A favorite magazine lying around can say, "I'm really glad you are here." You may decide to eat in the dining room, or serve freshly baked cookies or homemade bread. Little acts of thoughtfulness go a long way toward building healthy relationships and making someone feel comfortable.

This is also important when your mother- and father-in-law come to visit. I try to cook ahead when in-laws and parents are visiting. I'll never forget one Christmas when I left much to the last minute. As I was slaving in the kitchen trying to get it all together, my Dad kept asking Dave, "Where's Claudia?" In retrospect, I realize he would have enjoyed my company more than my labor—but then he did love to eat! If I had done a better job of preparing ahead, he could have experienced both. Now is the time to stop and think about what you can do to make the next visit with your in-laws more comfortable and relaxing.

One smart mother-in-law planned a family vacation around her son-in-law's favorite activity—playing golf. They all met at Palm Springs during the Bob Hope Golf Classic. Tickets for the event were waiting for her husband and lucky son-in-law. And she had planned other activities for her and her daughter.

Action: Ways to make your daughter- or son-in-law feel comfortable

- Observe special tastes and cater to them. Buy a favorite cereal, flavored coffee or tea, or vegetarian specialties.
- Have fresh flowers in the bedroom. You can even put a chocolate candy kiss on each pillow.
- Pick up his or her favorite reading material. One mother-in-law noticed that her son-in-law always read her *Reader's Digest,* so she made

sure one was always available when he visited. Later in talking to her daughter, she discovered that *Reader's Digest* wasn't his favorite—he just loved to read. The next visit, he found *The New York Times* and *Money Magazine* with the *Reader's Digest*!

7 ❖ Provide Adequate Sleeping Arrangements

It wasn't going to be a pleasant day. We could tell from the start. The problem wasn't the day, but the night before—you know, that time we were supposed to get our rest. Well, we didn't. The quaint Austrian hotel where we were staying had in the past been quiet and restful, but that night it was anything but quiet. The rowdy party of the century took place under our windows!

As we met our friends for breakfast, we could tell they had gotten less sleep than we did. Now we are very close friends, and we get along great. (You have to be that kind of friends to spend two weeks together traveling in a foreign country!) Still even with no agenda, no negatives, this day was tense. We just don't function as well without sleep. When you add the built-in tensions of family and in-laws to a lack of sleep, you have the potential for fireworks!

In-law relationships are hard to maintain, but they may be extra hard if you're tired and grouchy. That's why it's important to do what you can to provide adequate sleeping arrangements when your son or daughter and his or her spouse come to visit.

Attitude: *I will do all I can to provide privacy and a comfortable place to sleep when family members stay overnight.*

Do you remember the first time you visited your in-laws? I still remember the first time we visited my parents. We had only been married for two weeks. When we came downstairs for breakfast, one of my parents asked Dave if he had a good night. Dave was totally embarrassed. (It's one of the few times I remember Dave's face turning red!)

An in-law's visit is awkward enough, even if everything goes well. It's really awkward if you don't have adequate sleeping arrangements. Think about what you need to do to make their visits restful.

Action: *Ways to aid peaceful sleep*

- Check the condition of your guest bed if you have one. Sleep in it yourself one night. If you're not comfortable, that special couple won't be either. Consider putting a new bed and mattress into your budget.
- Check your pillows. Old musty pillows can keep guests awake and trigger allergies. We recently replaced our guest pillows with fresh ones for just twelve dollars.
- Purchase a comfortable sofa bed. Over the years, hide-a-beds have helped us utilize space and provide comfortable sleeping arrangements. But please try it out before you buy it. Once we slept on a sofa bed that almost permanently damaged our backs!

- Consider purchasing a three-inch-thick piece of foam rubber. On the floor it can be quite comfortable. When it's not in use, you can roll it up or store it under another bed.

8 ❈ Decide What You Want to Be Called (and It's Not "What's-Her-Name")

When I grew up in the South, the custom was to call mother-in-laws "Mother." As wonderful as Lillian is, I was never comfortable calling her "Mother." It was even harder to call Dave's father "Dad." So I usually called them nothing.

Years later it still puzzled me why this was so awkward. Then I got to the stage of life when I would soon be a mother-in-law. Looking at my relationship with Lillian, I appreciated her attitude that I was an adult—an equal, a friend. I never looked at her as my mother because I already had a wonderful mother.

I don't give up easily. Twenty-five years after marrying her son, I invited Lillian to lunch. I expressed my deep admiration and appreciation for her. No one could ever have a greater mother-in-law. Then I simply explained how I had felt awkward calling her Mom and asked if I could start calling her Lillian. Of course, she graciously said yes.

Learning from my experience with Lillian, I took the initiative and before our sons' weddings asked my future daughters-in-law to call me Claudia. It

helped from the start to establish more equal relationships—after all I'm not their mother!

Attitude: I want to be my in-law's peer and friend, not mother and authority figure.

You never will be his or her mother, nor do you
want to be. You've actively parented your son or
daughter. That role is over. Now is the time to "eat
your white bread" (as my mom says). Now is the
time to build a healthy *peer* relationship. It's never
too late. After all, it took me twenty-five years to figure it out.

Action: Ways to choose an appropriate name

*   Talk with your daughter- or son-in-law (or fu-
    ture in-law) about what you would like to be
    called. Get his or her input. What is comfort-
    able?
*   Choose a name that facilitates building a peer
    relationship.
*   *But I want to be called "Mom"!* If in your cul-
    ture (maybe you live in the South, too) you are
    comfortable being called Mom or Mother, go
    with it! If you have never had a child of that
    sex, you may especially want the identity of be-
    ing the mother of a son or daughter by being
    called Mom. It is not a right-or-wrong issue.
    The key is to find a name you are both happy
    with that encourages the relationship.

9 ❀ Communicate with Two

"All I was trying to do was to coordinate our family reunion. Instead I made a big, big mess." Rita made the reservations for the beach condo and checked with her daughter about dates, times, and what to bring. The only problem was that her daughter forgot to check with her husband. Picture in your mind the worst-case scenario and you will about have it.

Communication with in-laws is not what is said but what is heard—not just by one person but by two. Many times when we miscommunicate, we have only passed the message on to one—not two. So now, if it's something important, we try to talk as couples.

It's a greater challenge to communicate with two people than with one, but your daughter- or son-in-law will appreciate the extra effort. It will also earn you mother-in-law brownie points.

Attitude: I will seek to communicate with both, especially when it involves future plans together.

When communicating vital information, talk couple to couple. Remember, one-on-one times are great with our in-laws and sons and daughters, but be sen-

sitive when the information needs to get to both people. Don't assume that what is decided on by one will
be automatically OK with the other!

One seventy-five-year-old mother-in-law said she
tries to extend invitations through her daughter-in-
law instead of her son. This helps her not to take her
relationship with her son for granted. The tendency
is to go to your own son or daughter rather than
talking to them as a couple.

Once when we were making plans to attend a wedding, we talked to our son but not to our daughter-in-
law. We went on and made concrete plans which included other people. Not smart! It all worked out in
the end, but we could have avoided a few tense mo-
ments if we had talked to two people instead of one.

Action: Ways to communicate with both partners

- When you need a response, talk to both.
- Send a written confirmation if appropriate,
  such as, "We're looking forward to your visit
  this weekend."
- Don't be a go-between for other relatives or for
  your mate. Let them speak for themselves.
- Give them a speaker phone.

10 ❖ Give the Couple Adult Status

"Within two minutes, she reduced me to a ten year old!" Do you know that frustrating feeling? You feel very grown up. You should—you're over fifty and have married children yourself, but when you're around your mom, you instantly become the child.

My friend Millie laughingly told me about a recent conversation with her mother. "Millie, I just don't know what will ever happen to your brother," her mom said.

Millie responded, "Mom, he's fifty-eight years old. He's already happened!"

Millie and I both agreed we didn't want someday to be an eighty-three-year-old mother-in-law standing at the sink saying, "I don't know what will ever happen to my sixty-year-old son and daughter-in-law!" That's just not how we want to spend our twilight years—or for that matter, any year!

I know "the children" is an endearing term, but none of our adult offspring like to be called children. We don't like to be called children either!

Attitude: The job of parenting my adult daughter or son is over. I can now enjoy relating to this couple on an adult level.

While not calling them "the children" is a start, much more is involved in giving them adult status. You must acknowledge that they can vote, defend our country in war, have children, have their own bank accounts and credit cards, and sign contracts that you are not responsible for. Most adult children rise to the occasion and live responsible lives. If they don't, however, they are still adults.

Remember, you aren't responsible for what you can't control. Can you control your young married adults? The answer is no! Do you want to control your young married adults? The answer should be no! Then relax and repeat after me, "I give my son or daughter and his or her spouse adult status. I am not responsible for their decisions. My active parenting role is over. I can love, enjoy, accept, and appreciate relating to them as adults!"

Congratulations! You did it!

Action: Ways to affirm their adulthood

- Treat them as peers.
- Treat them as special guests. Now, I actually clean the house and plan special menus when our sons and their wives come to visit.
- Don't be a rescuer. Help only when asked and when you want to.

11 ❀ Develop Cultural Awareness and Sensitivity

"It wasn't until after we were married that I realized culture would be a major issue in my relationship with my mother-in-law." Lisa married into an American Japanese family. Her husband, Frank, seemed all-American. They got along great—it was Frank's mother whom Lisa found it hard to relate to. Lisa explained, "Frank's mother was interned during World War II. Her family lost everything they had and after the war had to start completely over. My mother-in-law to this day is fearful of losing everything again. That explains her tendency to be so obsessive-compulsive. For instance, she saves everything and hoards for the future. Her kitchen pantry looks like a bomb shelter for the whole town! She has enough food for an army. She also has enough clothes to dress a battalion. Many items are unused with the price tag still attached."

Lisa's advice is to try to understand your in-laws' culture. Once she understood how her mother-in-law grew up and how devastating it must have been to be interned right here in America, it helped her to be more tolerant and understanding.

Attitude: I will try to learn about, understand, and accept my daughter- or son-in-law's cultural background.

The world has gotten smaller. People travel and encounter many different cultures. There are more crosscultural marriages and, therefore, more cross-cultural in-laws. Recently we attended an American-Finnish wedding in Germany and it reminded us just how complicated crosscultural marriages can be. The ceremony was given in both English and Finnish so that all the in-laws and friends could understand— and that was just the wedding!

Even if your son- or daughter-in-law is the same nationality that you are, there may be other, more subtle cultural differences. Your in-laws may be from a different part of the country. Or they're contemporary, you're traditional; they're city, you're rural. Whatever the situation, you need to be aware and be sensitive.

Different cultures present different challenges. For instance, in the Chinese culture the husband's allegiance is first to his mother and then to his wife. If the mother-in-law holds this over the wife, storm clouds will develop. One wise Chinese mother-in-law said she had learned to let her son know his relationship with his wife had to come first—even if it did go against their culture. That's good advice for anyone.

Action: Ways to develop cultural awareness

- Research your in-law's family. What was his or her home like?

- Ask questions, such as, "How did you celebrate special occasions in your family?"
- Learn at least one ethnic recipe.
- Read books about his or her culture.
- Realize that your son or daughter and his or her spouse may develop their own unique way of life, and that's OK.

12 ✱ Keep Entertaining Simple

The first time we entertained my in-laws, we had only been married one week. Dave's parents were heading back to Naples, Italy, where they were stationed in the military, and stopped by our tiny basement apartment. Boy, was I nervous! I don't remember what I served them, but I do remember Lillian's accepting smile. She was just happy to be there. Food and how I served it were the least of her concerns.

Habits die hard. When our sons and daughters marry, they may take along the baggage: "This is the way Mom did it!" One of our sons even insisted his sandwiches be cut a certain way—the way Mom cut them.

How does your son- or daughter-in-law perceive you? Are you the totally awesome hostess? Can he or she measure up? What can you do to help your son- or daughter-in-law feel comfortable when his or her role is to entertain you?

***Attitude:** I desire to make my daughter- or son-in-law feel comfortable and adequate in her or his entertaining.*

A starting place is to keep your entertaining simple when your in-laws come to visit. One friend says each Christmas when her in-laws visit, she uses dessert plates or paper plates for sandwiches and serves Russian tea. She's quite a gourmet cook and could show off if she wanted to, but she says she would rather be a realistic model for her new daughter-in-law.

Remember to recognize your role in your adult children's home. You are now the guest. You'll get points for being a great mother-in-law if you respect their style, their taste, and their way of entertaining.

Action: Ways to be a realistic model when entertaining

- Get others involved. Assign chores and make sure everyone has a job—bring the dessert, fix the drinks, hold the baby, provide entertainment.
- Accept help from family members with a generous and thankful spirit.
- Use paper plates and napkins.
- Choose simple-to-prepare foods, such as cook-ahead casseroles, raw vegetables and dip (creamy Italian salad dressing makes great dip), or Stouffer's Frozen Lasagna (both meat and vegetarian are delicious and everyone will think you made it from scratch).
- Share these and other shortcuts with your in-laws.

13 ❋ Realize That Two Family Traditions Must Blend Together

"I'll never forget a conversation with Marcy the first Christmas season after she married my son, Rob," commented one mother-in-law. "Marcy called to ask how to make felt Christmas tree ornaments."

There's a history to this request. In discussing how to decorate their apartment for the holidays, Marcy asked her new husband, "What theme do you want for the Christmas tree—Victorian, English, or country?"

"Theme?" replied Rob. "You don't have a theme— you make everything."

As the mother-in-law, you can encourage the new family to choose traditions that are comfortable for them. Accept the fact that they will probably drop some of your favorite traditions, and that's OK. Others they will keep, and that's fun.

After the conversation with Marcy, my friend went through her tree decorations. Sure enough, they had made many of them as a family. She chose some that her son had made and others that were his favorites and sent them to Marcy and Rob. It was her little way of sharing some of the family's traditions with the next generation.

Attitude: *I choose to have no preconceived ideas of how my son or daughter and his or her spouse should celebrate holidays or carry on traditions. I will enjoy seeing their unique expression and will not be critical.*

It's only natural that you would desire to pass on traditions to the next generation, but when you try to force it, it becomes manipulation, and that's one tradition none of us wants to pass on.

There are unmanipulative ways to encourage them to continue family traditions. One of our favorite Christmas traditions is lighting the candles on our Austrian nativity pyramid. One year I found the same kind of pyramid on sale, so I bought three—one for each of our sons to have when they had their own home. This tradition was received with appreciation and gratitude.

Action: *Ways to encourage the blending of traditions*

- Pass on special mementos from childhood.
- Create a journal of traditions from your parents and grandparents. Include the ones you dropped—your offspring may want to pick them up!
- Repeat each day: "A rejection of my traditions is not a rejection of me."

14 ✤ Plan Realistically for Family Visits

Each year we get several Christmas cards from families who look like they are right out of the "Super Family Fairy Tale." Everyone is dressed alike and everyone is smiling. I admire them, but a picture like that just isn't realistic for us. Everyone in our family is so different, we would never agree on what to wear!

Even if we could pull off such a picture, it wouldn't reflect reality. I'm just happy when we get together and there are no major crises. Please don't misunderstand. I love it when we all can get together, especially when I resist adopting unrealistic expectations!

Evaluate your expectations. When the family gets together, what is the lowest common denominator? One friend told me, "When our married kids come back to visit, we're all adults for the first fifteen minutes. As the visit progresses, they regress and we get put back into the parent role. Not fun!"

Attitude: I willingly put aside my expectations and will look for ways to enhance our family time together.

For in-depth visits, it's best to get together couple-to-couple, but family reunions at Christmas and other times can be enjoyable, especially if we can put aside our expectations. (See Chapter 30 for suggestions for reunions and holidays.)

When the whole family visits, it's a good time to have the attitude of serving instead of being served. While you may not have time for in-depth conversations, your married children may. It's a time they can come together without the pressure of having to be the host and hostess. Try not to feel left out if this happens.

Action: Ways to facilitate happy family gatherings

- Apply no pressure for everyone to come. Command performances should be reserved for the military.
- Consider a neutral location. Suggest a cabin in the mountains or condo at the beach.
- Cook ahead.
- Be ready with family activities for those who want something to do. Plan a hike or a golfing outing, rent a couple of your family's favorite black and white videos, or pull out some puzzles or a few fun, favorite games. Recently at an Arp family gathering, we all had fun throwing darts and shooting pool.
- Give up any expectations of a *perfect* time together.

15 ❋ Share the Lighter Side of Life

There are times in life when you either have to laugh or to cry. If possible, choose to laugh. Laughter was our strategy for surviving the teenage years, and fortunately it became a habit.

Laughter is actually good for your health. It dispels tension, lowers your blood pressure, and may even improve your outlook on life. All these are assets where in-laws are concerned!

If we can look on the fun, lighter side of life, it will help to make our homes fun places for in-laws to visit. You can be sure there will be tense times in your relationships with your married children and their spouses. At these times, lighten things up.

I remember one Christmas one of our sons and his wife wanted to come visit with their cats. We had just finished remodeling parts of our house, including replacing the carpet. It really didn't suit to have cats visit so we said no.

They diffused tension in this situation by sending us a "Flat Cat." Our "Flat Cat" is a cardboard cat who lives on top of our refrigerator, requires no care except occasional dusting, and makes no messes, especially on our new carpet.

Attitude: I choose to look on the lighter side of life, and given the choice, I will laugh instead of cry.

Be willing to talk to your daughter- or son-in-law about the silly things you've done in the past. Share the humorous things that happen to you today as well as things that happened when you were first married. Choose to take life less seriously.

Action: Ways to lighten things up

- Inject humor into tense situations. Once I sent a card that showed a bear walking across a stage. It said, "Please bear with me. It's just a stage I'm going through!" You may want to visit a card shop and keep a supply of humorous cards. Hallmark has a great selection.
- Laugh together. Be willing to tell stories about silly things you did.
- Send humorous articles, cartoons, and other funny things of special interests.
- Pull out old scrapbooks. We made a scrapbook of all the things that were on our refrigerator as our boys were growing up. That's always good for a laugh or two.
- Buy a good joke book.

16 ❋ Stay Out of Their Finances

The world has changed in the years we have been married. Thirty years ago we were not tempted by instant credit and credit cards. There were none.

I can remember when our paycheck ran out before the end of the month. We'd head for the North Georgia mountains and spend a weekend with my parents. They graciously loved us, fed us, and let us use their washer and dryer. (Every load saved twenty-five cents!) As we were leaving, they usually loaded us up with groceries and wonderful home-canned beans and apple sauce. They never said that we were needy or made us feel guilty. They helped without getting involved in our finances.

While we have never lived near Dave's parents, I can't tell you the number of times Lillian was sensitive to our needs. Sometimes she slipped a crisp bill in a letter. It was never expected but always appreciated. By the way, she never asked about our finances.

Attitude: *I will not feel responsible for how my married children handle their finances. If I choose to help, I will do it in a way that will not foster dependency.*

How they spend their money is their concern, not yours. Before you become too critical, compare the world now with when you were first married. If we had had the option of credit cards and a line of credit at the bank, I'm not so sure we would have stayed out of debt. If you want to help, look for ways to help without producing guilt or indebtedness.

When my friend, Linda, visits her son and daughter-in-law, she goes grocery shopping with them. She is able to get a few necessities like caffeinated coffee and artificial sweetener (which this couple does not use) for herself, and she graciously picks up the tab for their groceries.

How can we help without incurring obligation to do the same thing the next time? It's not an easy question to answer, but it's worth thinking about.

Action: Ways to avoid interfering with their finances

- Ask no financial questions.
- Give no unsolicited advice.
- Don't compare your situation years ago to their situation now. You're not comparing apples with apples.
- Don't tempt them by suggesting that you go to the mall shopping together as a means of entertainment.
- Before doing anything (like cosigning or lending money) ask yourself, "Will this really help them or will it foster dependency?"

17 ❖ Call, but Not Too Often

The telephone is a blessing and a curse! Don't you just hate those telemarketing calls when you're just sitting down to dinner? On the other hand, good news often comes first over the telephone.

For a number of years we lived in Europe and the telephone was our link with parents and in-laws in the States. Little was as thrilling as a phone call from family—except when the call came in the middle of the night!

My father was Mr. Frugal, but he loved talking to us and would splurge from time to time on transatlantic phone calls. But he wasn't pleased when he got a baby-sitter on the other end instead of us. His solution? To call at 3 A.M. (European time) when the U.S. rates were low and he knew we would be at home. The problem with this was that by the time I was really awake, the conversation was over and I couldn't remember what had been said. Then I couldn't get back to sleep, so I was a grouch the next day. We can laugh about it today, but unfortunately most of those calls were counterproductive!

Attitude: I want to use the phone in such a way that when my son- or daughter-in-law hears my voice, he or she will be pleased.

One key we have found is to call, but not too often. If we are the only ones initiating the calls, we are probably calling too often. Also we try to be sensitive when they call us. The minutes are going on their phone bill instead of ours. Sometimes, in the past, we have even offered to call them back and make our own contribution to the phone company.

Also, be sensitive to their schedules. Middle-of-the-night calls are out! Other inappropriate times to call are during the evening news, during mealtime, and early in the morning when they are trying to get children off to school or walking out the door on their way to work.

Action: Ways to use the phone in a positive way

- If you get the answering machine, leave a brief message or hang up before the beep. To do otherwise is annoying. They know someone called them, but not who.
- Feel free to use your own answering machine when you don't want to be disturbed.
- Vary the times you call. Be unpredictable. Don't make it a ritual like the mother-in-law who for thirty years called every Sunday evening at 7 P.M.
- When you have nothing else to say, hang up.

18 ❈ Visit, but Not Too Often

Our friend Jim has a mother-in-law policy. She is a welcome guest in his home for the first twenty-four hours. Then he provides a comfortable motel room for her. It gives him and his wife the space they need, and Jim says it sure helps their relationship.

This might not work for you, but for Jim, who is a high-powered, hard-driving, family-loving man, it works. He likes to have his mother-in-law around for the short-term, but long-term visits are a problem.

Our best visits are the brief ones. Our philosophy is, "It is always better to leave and have them wish we had stayed longer than to overstay our welcome!"

When our sons were first married, we usually chose to stay at a nearby motel. It was a financial splurge, but it was an investment in healthy family relationships.

Attitude: My desire in visiting my son or daughter and his or her spouse is to build the relationship with them. I will keep my visits short and pleasant.

Before visiting, consider their living situation. If you stay with them, will you invade their privacy?

Will you create a financial burden? If they have children, will you disrupt their family routine? What can you do to make the visit more enjoyable for everyone?

If you are thinking over all these questions, you'll probably be a mother-in-law they will like to have around.

Action: *Ways to insure your visits will be positive*

- Take along what you need for your own comfort such as your own pillow or fan.
- If you like your cup of coffee the first thing in the morning, take your own little coffee pot. I have a small one that I keep in my overnight bag.
- Know when to go home!

19 ❋ Get to Know Your Son- or Daughter-in-Law's Parents

Our parents knew each other before Dave and I ever met. I remember telling my dad that I had a date with Dave Arp. His comment fascinated me: "If he's anything like his mother, he's really nice!"

Our lives have been enriched by getting to know the parents of our daughters-in-law. It's great if you can meet and get to know the parents of your son- or daughter-in-law, but it's not always easy to achieve. Maybe you live in California and your in-law's parents live in Maine. Visiting each other may not be feasible, but you can stay in touch through the telephone and the post office.

Maybe your in-law's parents live a little closer or business trips take you to their part of the world a couple of times each year. If it is possible to visit, it can be fun to see where your son- or daughter-in-law grew up and to look through family scrapbooks.

Times like these help us to connect and appreciate the unique past that influenced the wonderful person your child's spouse is today.

Attitude: I want to get to know my daughter- or son-in-law's family. I choose to love and accept them as part of our extended family and to complement and not compete with them.

My friend Jennifer made this commitment to her married children. She remembered the frustration she felt as a young mom trying to balance visits with two sets of parents who lived just a few minutes apart. The parents did not have much in common except expecting Jennifer and her family to spend priority time with them. However they tried to work it out, no one was pleased.

Perhaps if the parents had put forth more effort in building a relationship with each other it would have been easier for Jennifer to find balance. What is your situation? Do you have unrealistic expectations?

Action: Ways to get to know your daughter- or son-in-law's family

- Send pictures and little gifts from time to time. I've gotten some wonderful things in the mail, from sachets to Wisconsin cheese.
- Write a letter of appreciation. Tell them what you admire about their son or daughter.
- If you live close to each other, consider how you can coordinate schedules to make it easier for your married kids to spend time with both families.

20 ❖ Help with Household Chores, but Not Too Much

One young mom tells her story. "I was torn between wanting to stay home with my toddler and needing another source of income, at least temporarily. When my mother-in-law offered to come and stay with my son while I worked, it was a great encouragement to me. I was glad my son could remain in our home and be with someone he knew and loved.

"The only real problem was that my mother-in-law would also try to clean my house. When I got home from work, she was exhausted, but my house was spit-shined."

I asked this young mom how she felt. Her answer was, "Invaded, violated, inadequate, amazed, thankful, and appreciative with a slight twitch." It's not easy to find balance.

This made me stop and think about my past actions. Had I "overhelped" my daughters-in-law? What was my attitude? It was time to reevaluate.

Attitude: *I want to be sensitive to how I can help without overstepping and making my son- or daughter-in-law feel inadequate.*

Two times when I may have overdone it stand out in my memory. One was when we stayed in our son and daughter-in-law's vacant apartment for a little getaway. Before we left, we got the brainy idea to do a major cleaning for them. We were minimaids. We scrubbed, vacuumed, waxed the furniture, and even dried the stainless steel sink. The apartment sparkled!

The second time was when another son and daughter-in-law moved into their first home. We visited and offered to be their slaves for several days. Our first assignment was to help unpack boxes and clean the living room and dining room. We worked so hard our backs hurt.

I checked and both of our "helping out times" were appreciated and didn't produce any negative reactions, but we could have unsuspectingly communicated a different message.

Action: Ways to help with chores

- Ask what you can do to help and take the cue from them.
- Give a gift of a one-time maid service.
- If you can afford it, upgrade their vacuum cleaner if the one they have is an antique.
- Realize that sometimes they may say no when they really want the help. Be sensitive. Read the nonverbal clues!

21 ❧ Get a Life of Your Own

Did you hear the story about the elderly couple who in their nineties got a divorce? When asked why they waited so long, they replied, "We were waiting for all our children to die."

Believe it or not, some mothers-in-law are so tied to their children, they refuse to get a life of their own. This attitude doesn't make a great mother-in-law. No one needs a maternal figure hovering overhead like a helicopter, and no one needs to feel responsible for their mother-in-law's personal happiness.

Don't allow yourself to be too dependent on your married children and their spouses. It's not good for you or for them. Look for ways to build your own supportive friendships and to grow as a person. Enjoy the fact that your active parenting years are over!

Attitude: My son or daughter's first priority is now to their spouse and children. He or she does not love me less, but I am not the focal point of his or her life. I choose to continue to grow as a person and to develop new interests. I want a life of my own!

This attitude is much easier to maintain if you are

enjoying the empty nest. But at some point, you may begin to feel lonely. When Beth and Hal's children were grown and married, they moved to another part of the country. For the first couple of years, it was an adventure. They remodeled their 1930s home and enjoyed having time to get back into tennis and boating. But eventually they missed the kids, so to build their friendship circle, they started inviting others over for dinner.

Together they planned the menus and grocery shopped. Since they were both still working, they found shortcuts such as prepared sauces for their gourmet entrees. They discovered they actually enjoyed entertaining, and a whole new world opened up for them. They still miss their adult children and are thrilled when they visit, but at other times they have their own life and their own friends.

If your life is lonely, let me encourage you to look outward. We all share difficult circumstances. Everyone has problems of one sort or another. The choice is yours—to concentrate on your problems or to expand your world. Perhaps now is the time to "get a life."

While you value your past, think now about how you can improve your future. Begin by taking a personal inventory. What relationships do you enjoy? Is there something you used to do that you enjoyed? Whatever you did before, now you may be able to do it better. I know one lady who, at sixty-nine years old, bought a piano at a garage sale. Six years later she bought a baby grand piano and, now in her late eighties, practices two hours each day. She even plays for weddings and other special events.

Action: Ways to build your own life and expand your world

- Start a new hobby. Use your home as your workshop. Mess it up yourself. The kids did— now it's your turn. Paint, write, garden, or whatever suits your fancy.
- Take the initiative in developing new friends. Join clubs and organizations, volunteer for community service, learn a new sport.
- List things you enjoy. What makes a day worthwhile? A walk? *The New York Times?* A phone call? Perhaps you enjoy bird watching or traveling. Make time for the things that fulfill you.

22 ❋ Find Things in Common

The big "Five-O" was approaching me, and our sons and daughters-in-law wanted to do something special to celebrate. Since they didn't have the financial means to send us on a European vacation, we settled on a small dinner party. The real gift to me was seeing them pull off a delicious five-course dinner and having our friends get to know them better and vice versa.

To help develop a sense of belonging, look for things you have in common. Everyone has to eat, so food is one shared interest. One mother-in-law gave this advice: if you're bored, learn a new recipe together. She still laughs about cooking with her daughter-in-law. Together they made a casserole and it was a total flop. Her solution? To make the dried-out rice and vegetable casserole edible, she simply melted a stick of butter and poured it over the casserole. Voilà! It tasted great! If only all in-law relationships could be improved by melting a stick of butter. (Since I heard this story, I've resorted to the butter treatment for turkey dressing that's too dry. It definitely improves the flavor!)

Attitude: *I choose to continually look for things we have in common and to build a genuine friendship through doing things together.*

Look for things you have in common or *could* have in common. For instance, years ago when our boys were growing up, one Christmas we all got Austrian wool bedroom slippers. They were so toasty and warm that we continued the tradition over the years. When one pair wore out, we simply replaced them with a new pair. When one of our sons was married in Austria, the tradition was extended to our daughters-in-law. It's nice to know our feet all look alike.

Another time I gave each couple a homemade cookbook of our family's favorite recipes including Grandmother Arp's pumpkin pie, my mom's molasses cookies, Aunt Myrtle's coconut cake, and my favorite cheese fondue recipe.

Whatever your interest, whatever the interest of your daughter- or son-in-law, look for commonality. It will enhance your relationship.

Action: *Ways to develop a sense of belonging and commonality*

- Host a dinner party together. It's fun to cook together. Try new recipes.
- Choose a family project, at your house or theirs, such as wallpapering a room or putting up shelving in a closet. Do it together.
- Take a vacation together. Once we went to Disney World with my parents. It wasn't their first

choice of places to visit, but the grandkids loved Disney World and getting to experience it with their grandparents. We all built great memories.

- Play games together. Some of our favorite are Scattergories, Balderdash, and Pictionary.

23 ❖ Ask for Advice

"We had only been married for two weeks when we visited Bill's parents," said Camilla. "Imagine my surprise when Bill's mother asked me how he wanted his eggs fixed! She had fixed his breakfast for over twenty years, yet she deferred to me."

Camilla told her mother-in-law the only way she had fixed eggs for Bill so far was "burned." Bill's mother just smiled. She was already off to a great start as a mother-in-law by stepping back and deferring to her new daughter-in-law.

Now, Camilla is a mother-in-law and is practicing what she learned from Bill's mother. Part of deferring to her daughter-in-law is having an attitude of "letting go." She watches what she says and chooses to pray into existence rather than to talk into existence. Whenever it's appropriate, she asks her daughter-in-law for advice or for her opinion.

Attitude: *I will choose to defer to my son- or daughter-in-law and will not make assumptions. When appropriate, I will ask for advice or an opinion.*

I've gotten some good suggestions and advice by

asking my daughters-in-law their thoughts and opinions. I've even learned new things about my sons. People change and their choices also may change. Don't assume you know your own son's or daughter's preferences. Our family grew up never using pepper. Now, one of our sons likes food with his pepper. Another son is slowly becoming a vegetarian.

My mother-in-law, Lillian, has always been a great example of "letting go." She loves to hear about our life and has always deferred to me in a graceful way. She has helped me realize that I may not know as much about my own sons as I think I do. As we grow older we change, and often our tastes change as well. Your son- or daughter-in-law can be a great source for updating personal data about your own child.

Action: Ways to defer to my son- or daughter-in-law

- Listen attentively when he or she shares an opinion.
- Ask for suggestions.
- Ask questions.
- Recognize that your children's tastes and styles may change as they grow older and their spouses may now know them better than you do.
- Don't assume anything!

24 ✿ Encourage Adventure and Creative Dating

Remember when you were first married? Everything was an adventure. But if you were like most couples, before long you settled into a rather predictable routine. Dating became something you did *before* you were married.

Sometimes young married couples don't date or expand their horizons because of a lack of resources or a lack of time. A little nudge from a caring mother-in-law can make a big difference. My friend Jane is a mother-in-law to three. When her youngest daughter married while still in college, she decided to give the newly married couple a challenge.

Jane is a firm believer in the value of education through participation in purposeful activity. She wanted to encourage her daughter and son-in-law to continue having new experiences, so she offered them a contract for creative dating. She would finance their dates if they would try new things. The contract included one date every other month and a dollar limit.

Did it work? Jane says yes. One month they went to an Ethiopian restaurant, another time to a disco. The contract definitely encouraged some creative dates that perhaps they would have never experienced otherwise.

Attitude: **I will look for ways to encourage my married children and their spouses to have new experiences, expand their horizons, and enjoy each other.**

One way to encourage the next generation to seek new adventures is to be adventurous yourself. Never underestimate the power of your example. We want to keep growing and learning new things as long as we live. Just recently, Dave and I learned how to cross-country ski. New experiences keep us growing and expanding and will do the same for our married children.

Action: **Ways to encourage expanding horizons and adventure**

- Finance creative dates. Offer a challenge: encourage them to take a risk, to experience something new, or to go on an educational date. Suggest that they go backpacking, try dinner at an Indian restaurant, or learn French together. Include with your challenge a dollar limit and a time frame.
- Give a gift of time—your time to baby-sit.
- Give a subscription to a unique magazine or educational journal.
- For other fun dating suggestions, you may want to give them a copy of *52 Dates for You and Your Mate* (Nashville: Thomas Nelson, 1993).

25 ❧ Listen, Listen, Listen

"I would have a better relationship with my mother-in-law if she would just listen and be interested in our life," Karen commented. "It's like talking to a blank wall. I could tell her anything and she would just say, 'That's nice.' What can I do to make her listen to me?"

Unfortunately, there is nothing Karen can do to make her mother-in-law listen. But as the mother-in-law, there is much you can do to insure that you are listening to your son- or daughter-in-law. Listening begins with a desire to hear what someone else is saying. It starts with the assumption that you are genuinely interested in the person talking. Effective listening is as much an attitude as an action.

Attitude: *I choose to be interested in my son- or daughter-in-law, to really listen to what he or she says, and to seek to understand what he or she means by what is said.*

Good communication is not just hearing what other people say, but understanding what they mean by what they say. It involves asking appropriate questions and listening closely to the answers. Listen for the nonverbal as well as the verbal message. According to a Kodak study, the words that we speak are only 7 percent of the total message. Nonverbal clues —that's the stares and glares and body language— account for 55 percent of the message, and tone of voice—the way we say it—is a surprising 38 percent of the message. There is much more to listen to than mere words. The next time you talk to your in-law, be aware of the total message. You may hear much more!

Action: Ways to listen better to your in-law

- Listen to what is not being said. Ask questions and listen to the answers.
- Watch your own nonverbal communication and tone of voice.
- Complete the communication cycle by saying "This is what I hear you saying." Then repeat what you heard so you're satisfied that you are hearing what he or she is really trying to say.

26 ❋ Consider Finances When You Visit or Travel Together

One thing we loved about living in Europe was the opportunity to travel, especially when family could visit and join us. These trips could have been a financial nightmare, but my in-laws and parents helped in a way that didn't produce guilt.

One particular visit stands out in my mind. It was May, the flowers were beginning to bloom, the weather for Austria was fantastic, and our three sons were enjoying their grandparents.

As we took short trips together, they made traveling together fun and economical for us by introducing us to the "travel kitty." Each relative put equal amounts of money into the kitty. Sometimes we were allowed to participate but not this particular time. (The dollar in relation to the Austrian shilling was extremely low and our finances were tight!) The kitty paid all the common bills like gas, tolls, food, and motels. We were able to introduce them to Europe without incurring a financial headache in the process.

***Attitude:** I want to be sensitive to my married children's financial situation when I visit and travel with them. I will look for ways to help without being obvious or creating obligation.*

You have the choice. Choose not to be a financial burden. Consider helping with groceries. One friend told me it's less awkward to go to the grocery store with your own son or daughter if possible.

Also be sensitive to their eating habits. They don't need to spend extra money on food they normally would not buy. So if you need bran cereal or decaffeinated coffee, buy your own; or better still, bring it from home!

Another friend gives her married children and their spouses plane tickets for Christmas and birthdays. If your children live far away (more than one day's travel time by car), plane tickets can be a gift they will enjoy receiving. My friend travels often in her business and collects free certificates that can be used by other family members. Also, watch for airfare wars. We've even found two-for-one tickets from time to time.

***Action:** Ways to help financially when you visit and travel together*

- Travel with a well-fed "kitty."
- Feel free to bring gifts of things you know they need or especially want.
- Offer to help with a project or need. If towels

are sparse, make new towels a hostess gift. One mother-in-law always gives new washcloths when she visits. Then she knows she will always have one to use.

27 ❀ Remember That You Have at Least One Thing in Common

Recently I attended a bridal luncheon for the daughter of one of my best friends. After a delicious brunch each guest was asked to give the bride one tip for getting along with her future mother-in-law. Since I was in the process of researching *52 Ways to Be a Great Mother-in-Law,* I wanted to say something really profound, but the one thing that stood out in my mind was this tip: "Remember you will always have one thing in common—you both love the same person." This advice can be a great help when there are many other areas where you disagree.

One daughter-in-law related how she tried for twenty years to relate to her mother-in-law but never felt accepted or respected. After twenty years, her mother-in-law finally began to come around, and today they have a pleasant relationship. If you are the mother-in-law struggling with a daughter-in-law who is totally different from you, you can help build mutual respect by remembering what you do have in common—you both love your son—and it won't take twenty years to build a relationship. Then look for other things you have in common. You may be surprised by what you find.

Attitude: *Whatever our differences, we both love the same person. I will remember that he or she loves my daughter or son and be grateful. I will also concentrate on what we have in common, not on areas where we disagree.*

It's your choice. You can concentrate on the positive things you see in your in-law, or you can dwell on the negative. Why not take a few minutes and make a list of all the positive traits you can think of that describe your daughter- or son-in-law. You may even admire some of the ways he or she is totally different from you. Each person is unique and it's up to you to appreciate that uniqueness, especially when it comes to your in-laws.

Action: *Ways to build respect and look for things you have in common with your son- or daughter-in-law*

- Compliment your in-law in the presence of your son or daughter and vice-versa. Most people like to be affirmed in the presence of their mate.
- Make a list of your daughter- or son-in-law's positive qualities.
- Make a list of ways you are different that give variety to your family tree.
- Affirm the growing edges you see. Is your son-

or daughter-in-law attempting something new? Is he or she taking a risk to grow in an area— maybe learning a new sport, trying low-fat cooking, trying to lose that extra ten pounds, or working out? Is he or she bravely switching jobs or professions to something better suited and more fulfilling?

28 ❀ Build Your Own Marriage

"What do we do now that our children are grown?" asked one mom. We were speaking to a group of parents who were entering the empty nest stage of family life and one big concern surfaced. Many had little in common with the other bird left in their empty nest. It was as if their marriage relationship had hibernated until their children grew up and married. Their children had been the focus of their family life, and the temptation now was to be over-involved in the lives of their married adult children.

Maybe one reason Lillian has always related to me in such a healthy way is that she focused on building her own marriage, not on being overinvolved in ours. When your own marriage is sour, it's easy to become emotionally dependent on your adult children and their spouses. If you are single at this stage of life, it's time to build positive relationships with other adults. It's time to broaden your horizons to include people other than your offspring.

Attitude: *I choose to focus on my mate and other adult friends and not on my son or daughter and his or her spouse. I choose to do all I can to enrich my marriage.*

You may be a mother-in-law who still has younger children at home. It's never too early, even for you, to begin planning for enriching your marriage when the nest empties. For years we talked about taking a trip to New England the autumn after all our sons had left home, and it actually happened. The trip allowed us to set fresh goals for our marriage and enjoy being just two again.

A word to the wise: don't wait until your children grow up to build your marriage. Now is the time to build for the future. Look at the time you have right now and use it. As we did, your married children will benefit from a parental model of a healthy love relationship.

Action: Ways to build your own marriage

- Start dating your mate. Plan a date with your mate for this week.
- Plan a twenty-four-hour getaway for two.
- Read a book on marriage, such as *The Marriage Track* (Nashville: Thomas Nelson, 1992), or *60 One-Minute Marriage Builders* (Nashville: Thomas Nelson, 1993).
- Sit down with your husband over a cup of coffee or tea and talk about your hopes and dreams. Don't talk about your kids and in-laws.

29 ❈ Spend Time Alone with Your Daughter- or Son-in-Law

With some, it just happens. It seems natural to go for a walk, shopping, or out to lunch together. Time together tends to be relaxed and enjoyable. With others, it may not be as easy or natural to spend time together.

I'll never forget the first time I was alone with one of my daughters-in-law. We made a quick trip to a discount warehouse and got caught in a huge storm. As we were checking out, the electricity went out, so she offered to go get the car. It was raining so hard I just jumped in the car on the passenger side, and she had to drive home through uncharted waters. There was no tension being together—the storm provided another avenue of stress.

***Attitude:** I will look for natural opportunities to spend time alone with my son- or daughter-in-law. My desire is to get to know him or her, to develop trust between us, and to build a relaxed, positive relationship.*

Occasionally, seek time alone with your son- or daughter-in-law. Just-you-and-me times are great if they happen naturally, but you shouldn't force it. If it becomes something that is expected, then it becomes manipulation and it's unhealthy for the relationship.

Also, creating opportunities to spend time together is easier with a daughter-in-law than with a son-in-law. Often a son-in-law likes watching football or fishing, and those activities may not be your strong suits. It may be awkward to invite your son-in-law out to lunch, but you might enjoy chatting over a cup of coffee in the kitchen.

The telephone offers a great way to have one-on-one conversations. My friend Barbara says that some of her best conversations with her son-in-law occur when she calls and he answers. They may talk for several minutes and even tease her daughter, "Hey, in a few minutes we'll let you talk!" So the next time your son- or daughter-in-law answers the phone, don't be so quick to connect with your own son or daughter.

Remember, there is a balance between desiring to spend time with someone and ignoring him or her. You don't want your in-law to feel pressured into just-you-and-me times, but on the other hand, you don't want him or her to feel you're not interested in spending time together.

Action: Ways to spend one-on-one time

- Take advantage of spontaneous times that just happen. Start a conversation when you're both in the kitchen getting something to drink or sitting down to watch the evening news. If you're both night owls or day larks, take advantage of the time when everyone else is asleep.

- Invite your in-law out to lunch. In a neutral setting it may be easier to relate to each other. Lunch in a nice café can put both of you on your best behavior.
- Walk around the block together.
- Go along to the grocery store (with your checkbook).

30 ✿ Plan for Family Reunions and Holidays

"This was the first Christmas we didn't have tears," said one of my friends who has had married children come to visit the last five Christmases. I didn't really understand until we had married kids of our own, but now I know it's not all joy, togetherness, and pumpkin pie.

Family reunions and holidays can get on your nerves. When the family comes from far and near, inlaw relationships can soar or sour. As the mother-in-law, you are a key player and can do some things to help these times be a positive experience, but you can't make it happen!

"I love my family, but sometimes I just can't deal with them when they are all around." Rhonda continued, "When we all get together, I overeat, and conflicts I thought were long buried seem to resurface. Why can't we have one really pleasant, conflict-free family reunion?"

Can you identify with Rhonda? Why do we expect holidays and family reunions always to be happy times for everybody? When families get together, they usually run into some conflicts with each other. Sometimes these arguments are the result of old conflicts that have never been resolved. It's easy to revert to former ways of thinking when we get together as families. What can we do as mothers-in-law to help make these times more positive than negative? We can start with our own attitudes.

Attitude: *I will resist the tendency to have inflated expectations when the whole family gets together for special occasions. I will also realize that with time holidays and reunions can become easier.*

Whatever your situation at family get-togethers, there will be some things that never change and other things that over time can improve. It helps tremendously if you can have a more realistic and accepting attitude toward these family times. Family reunions are not a production with you as the producer. There are so many variables and so many personalities involved—often you just have to go with the flow. Realize it's OK to have some conflict, disagreement, and expression of feelings. The good news is that as you get older, family times together will become easier. As the mother-in-law, your job isn't to keep everyone happy, but there are some things you can do to cope.

Action: *Ways to survive family get-togethers*

- Spend time beforehand thinking through the upcoming time together. Make a list of things you can do ahead of time.
- Realize that you can't control other people.
- During the family get-together, take time for

yourself. Read a book. Take a nap. Get away from everyone for a couple of hours—it'll help your perspective!

- Get some exercise. Walk around the block.
- Don't be the family arbitrator.
- Let everyone help out in the kitchen. Ask for help if no one volunteers.
- Realize that soon everyone will go home!

31 ❈ Respect Your Own Son or Daughter

"When our married kids come to visit, I'm just the sweetest little thing that ever came down the pike." Kathy went on to explain. "I try to be extra nice not only to my daughter-in-law, but also to my son. When they have children, I want access to my grandchildren, and one way I can assure that is to treat my son like Sir Lancelot and my daughter-in-law like a princess."

We all need reminders to treat our own son or daughter with respect. Why is it that sometimes it's easier to be more kind and considerate to those we hardly know—like the checker at the grocery store or the stranger we meet in a restaurant—than to our own flesh and blood? Stop and think about all the wonderful things about your son or daughter. Then meditate on them.

Attitude: *I want my son or daughter to feel cherished and to know that he or she is loved.*

"It's not that I don't love and appreciate my daughter, it's just that I forget to ever tell her." This mom needs to practice being verbal in affirming her daughter.

If you have difficulty finding the lovely things about your son or daughter—their quirks drive you crazy—stop for a moment and pretend that he or she is in someone else's family. You may be able to laugh away the little irritations. Certainly, you won't take things so seriously.

Remember, your child has a world too. When you are really close to your son or daughter it's easy to overstep. My friend Suzie related a recent conversation with her mom. Now that Suzie has a baby, her mom just can't stay away. They have a great relationship and enjoy being together, but one day when Suzie's mom asked her to stop by Suzie responded, "Mom, I just can't."

Her mom answered, "What? Do you mean you have a life of your own?" They both laughed. Together they are finding the balance of loving and appreciating each other and at the same time finding a life of their own. One thing is certain. Suzie feels loved and respected as an adult, a daughter, and a mother.

Action: Ways to show your son or daughter that he or she is special

- Be really interested in his or her world. Ask questions and really listen to the answers.
- Learn about the things your son or daughter is interested in. One mother whose daughter switched her musical preference from classical to country spent hours at the record shop learning who's who in country music.

- Do what you can to build an adult friendship with your son or daughter.
- Never, never criticize your son or daughter in front of his or her mate.
- Write a personal letter to just your son or daughter and express your love and confidence in him or her. Describe what you appreciate about your child.

32 ✿ Keep Your Perspective When You Have to Live Under the Same Roof

What do you do when your comfortable empty nest begins to refill with adult children, in-laws, and maybe even grandchildren? One friend said, "Leave home!"

In many cultures, several generations of families live together. In the past, this was often the case in our culture. For the first year of my parent's marriage, they lived with my grandmother. In-law relationships are hard to maintain in a normal setting, and they can be extra stressful when you must temporarily live together. However, there are situations today when you may need to make room in your nest. When this happens, how can you make the best of it? You can start with looking at your attitude.

Attitude: I choose to do what I can to make this time harmonious and pleasant, and to be flexible when I can while finding balance in what I can and cannot do.

You can handle stress better when you realize,

"This is temporary" and when at least one other person understands how you feel. If you have a supportive mate, great. If not, find a friend who will be willing to listen and to encourage you. Some bicycles are built for two, but few houses are adequate for two generations. However, my friend Janet tells me it can be a positive, growing experience. Janet does suggest having a game plan, setting specific guidelines. If there are grandchildren, include baby-sitting arrangements.

When adult children come home to roost with in-laws and sometimes grandchildren, it's easy for them to slip back into the child role. Never having personally experienced this, I asked others who have for suggestions. The best advice I've gotten is to "talk, talk, talk!" and to "listen, listen, listen!"

Together work out guidelines for financial arrangements, household chores, rules for pets. (Yes, some bring a menagerie of animals.) You may want to renegotiate each month and set a time of evaluation to ask, "How is this working?"

Then, remind yourself why you are doing this. It may be a way to help your offspring temporarily. If it's permanent, do what you can to give each family privacy and breathing space. Don't be a doormat or a dictator. Balance is there. Find it—your future relationship depends on it!

Action: Ways to make living with in-laws work

- Keep your sense of humor and be flexible.
- Talk and listen to each other. Have planned

times of communication. You may decide you will touch base each Monday evening and resolve any issues.

- Set reasonable house rules—like you get it out, you put it back. You mess the kitchen, you clean the kitchen.
- Write down guidelines and financial arrangements so there are no misunderstandings about what was agreed upon.
- Respect each other's privacy.
- Together talk about what each person needs most to make this work. ("I need a living room without clutter." "I need real coffee in the morning." "I need a time to relax and play the piano." "I need space.")

33 ✽ Respect Their Decisions

I've done some crazy things in my thirty years of marriage, but I can never remember Lillian criticizing or giving unsolicited advice. I remember once when we made a drastic job change. Dave completely changed professions, going from a job in the computer industry with financial security to full-time Christian work with little financial security but much more personal fulfillment. Most people thought we had lost our minds, but Lillian remained supportive and even kept our young children so we could attend a training conference on the West Coast.

It's not always easy to accept our adult children's decisions. It's just as difficult to have our own parents question ours—that's what a friend recently expressed to me. "I just can't tell my mother-in-law I'm pregnant again. She had a fit when Callie was born, and now we're having our fourth child!"

My friend continued, "We always wanted a large family, but my husband came from the 'two children is the perfect number' mold, and his mom is really upset!"

Another friend related how upset her mother-in-law is that she and her husband joined a different church denomination. "She just doesn't realize that this is the church that is meeting our needs and where we are comfortable. She thinks we're raising her grandchild to be a heathen."

Attitude: I will respect my adult children's decisions. I will not interfere or criticize.

You don't have to look very far to find strained in-law relationships. We have different life perspectives, and even if our values are similar, there are probably shades of difference. Now look at your own family and check out how well you are doing at accepting your adult children and their spouses. If you need help, repeat the attitude statement above!

We all must deal with the fact that it's their life. We had approximately eighteen years to pass on our values. Now it's their call. If in the past we haven't let go, now is the time. You may be surprised how freeing this can be.

Action: Ways to resist interfering and to accept their value judgments

- Delay forming strong opinions. However well you think you understand their situation, you don't have all the facts and it is *their situation*.
- Learn how to put on a "poker face."
- Do not volunteer your opinion.

34 ❖ Learn to Laugh Together and Cry Together

Sometimes there is a fine line between laughter and tears. Both can help blend families together, and both will happen when we are vulnerable and real with each other. We have always laughed a lot in our family; tears are more rare. One time we did cry together. It was a couple of years ago when my dad passed away.

All our sons and daughters-in-law came from different parts of the United States, even though it was a very inconvenient time. Just watching the way they swung into action to support their mom gave me strength. They let me be real. We cried together, and we reminisced and talked until the wee hours of the morning. In our sorrow, we even found laughter as we talked about Father and all his wonderful antics, like the fruitcakes he used to make and his trying to tune the piano—he always thought he could do anything! In my vulnerability, I found comfort and closeness that to this day is a precious memory.

Other times in our life, we have roared with laughter. One time on my birthday we played "Claudia Trivia" with categories like "Claudisms" and "Name that Book." "Claudisms" were my favorite sayings, like "It takes a little insanity to keep our sanity" and

"You have so much potential." The "Name that Book" category included quotes from books I had written that were taken totally out of context—to make me look ridiculous, of course!

Attitude: *I will share my emotions, from laughter to tears. I will be real.*

When we hurt, it is OK to say so. One friend shared with me how her daughter and son-in-law expected to be remembered on their birthdays but often forgot hers. So once she simply ignored their birthdays. They were extremely hurt until they realized, "Hey, we've been doing the same thing!"

It can build relationships when you are willing to be real. When you feel like someone is overwhelmed, let him or her know you've been there before. Ask yourself what you can do to give that person a reprieve.

Action: *Ways to promote the sharing of life's laughter and tears*

- Give comfort and share joy through cards and notes. When my dad passed away, the most comforting note I received was from someone who simply wrote a few lines but who was able to identify with my loss.
- Refuse to assign blame.
- When someone hits a rough spot, help him or her get back on track. Think about what you can do to help.
- Know the difference between tension and sor-

row. Joking may relieve tension, but it may be inappropriate when someone is grieving a loss.

- Plan a fun family event. Ask each couple to prepare a skit or bring their favorite game or silly reading. We still read from the book *Where the Sidewalk Ends* by Shel Silverstein.
- Remember your child's anniversary.

35 ❋ Acknowledge That Love Is a Choice

"I try to talk to my daughter-in-law, and all I get is a polite yes or no," related one mother-in-law. "I want to have the same warm relationship I have with my other in-laws, but she just won't let it happen."

If you relate to this mother-in-law, stop for a moment and think about your expectations. Are you trying to force your unresponsive in-law into the same mold as your other in-laws? Each person is a unique individual. Realize that some relationships are going to be closer than others. Maybe it's time to step back, look at your expectations, and give a little space.

What about the daughter- or son-in-law who is indifferent to you? You try to reach out, and it's as if you bump into a stone wall. You get no response at all. In a situation like this, you need to remember that love is a choice—a choice you can make as an act of love to your own son or daughter.

***Attitude:** I choose to love my daughter- or son-in-law—to look realistically at our relationship and to do what I can to improve it.*

While some things may improve over time, other things are a given. You will not be able to change your in-law's personality or irritating habits, but you may be able to change your own response. Maybe it's time to reflect. Have you done something to offend your daughter- or son-in-law? Is there a present conflict that is causing tension in your relationship? Maybe you disapprove of his childrearing techniques, her life-style, or how she spends her money. Is there something you know you need to ask forgiveness for? Do you need to give more space in the relationship?

Action: Ways to choose to love your son- or daughter-in-law

- Give space in the relationship. Don't call as often; don't visit as frequently; don't ask too many questions.
- Ask forgiveness if you have offended him or her.
- If your expectations aren't realistic, get rid of them.
- Realize this is your son's or daughter's choice of mate and be determined to look for the positive.

36 ✱ Remember, We All Have to Eat

I grew up in the Old South where food was life itself. The whole day revolved around the words, "When do we eat?" Dave's Grandmother Arp ran a hotel. Meals there were incredible! Once I counted thirteen vegetables and four meats—all in the same meal. That could have been a whole week's menu at our house!

Food influences family relationships. We all have to eat, and with in-laws mealtimes can be positive or negative. It's something to think about.

One way I have discovered how to be a great mother-in-law is to turn the kitchen over to the younger generation when they are visiting. Dave and I are easy to please, so we let our married couples plan the menu and grocery shop (we try to cover the grocery bill). Then I get out of their way!

Not only do they take pride in their culinary skills, they serve their meals with creative flair. Once they decided the dining room table needed to be extended farther than our dining room allowed, so they simply moved the table into our den. The ambience was wonderful. It was like being in a tiny French restaurant. By the way, they returned my dining room table to its original home, but only after a memorable dinner in the den.

Attitude: *I will strive to use food to bless, to enhance, and to facilitate great communication, not as a weapon or secret tool of manipulation.*

Try to remember likes and dislikes. It's not necessary or advisable to cater to every little whim, but your son- or daughter-in-law will appreciate your thoughtfulness in having sugar substitute, decaffeinated coffee, skim milk, or his or her favorite brownies.

Our married kids cook with less pepper when we visit because they know we don't like things extremely spicy. When they visit us, they appreciate our having extra pepper on the table so they can spice up their food.

Action: *Ways to use food to bless and facilitate great relationships*

- Prepare food ahead of time to avoid feeling like a martyr.
- Let meals be a family affair. Recruit and accept offers of help.
- Respect food preferences without making them a major issue.
- When you're too exhausted to cook, and no one else wants to cook, call for pizza or your favorite take out.

37 ❀ Let Them Parent Their Own Children

It's hard enough to be a parent. It's even harder if there's a mother-in-law watching and waiting for you to mess up. One young mom shared her frustration. Her mother-in-law kept her three-year-old son for the weekend. When she picked him up, her mother-in-law had washed *and* ironed all of his clothes, including underwear and t-shirts! And she had written out detailed instructions for how to wash her grandson's clothes, including details such as "turn clothes inside out before placing in the washing machine." This mom wanted to turn her mother-in-law inside out. You can be sure she did turn off the relationship.

Attitude: *I want to enjoy grandchildren—not evaluate them. I have parented my children; my job is over.*

One mother-in-law I know spends most of her time worrying about her grandson. She disapproves of how her daughter-in-law is choosing to raise him and just knows he will end up being a juvenile delinquent. Another grandmother worries about a granddaughter who is in her thirties.

What about baby-sitting? My good friend who has five grandchildren has charted her own course. Her advice is, "Keep kids if it's convenient and if you want to do so. But, remember, being a martyr will not build your relationship with your grandchildren or your daughter- or son-in-law."

I don't know what kind of grandmother I will be, but I'm looking forward to becoming one. I know there is room for creativity. I do hope to be caring, not coercive; merry, not a martyr! Lillian has been a great role model. To this day, she never criticizes her grandchildren. She was always happy to see our family but never pressured us to visit. Once she even went beyond the call of duty and kept two preschoolers for two weeks.

Action: Ways to be a supportive grandmother

- Spend time with your grandchildren without their parents around.
- Plan just-me-and-Grandma times with each grandchild.
- Listen to your grandchildren—they are fascinating people!
- Enrich their lives with your experiences and talents. If you play a musical instrument, give music lessons if they are interested.
- Go to their performances such as plays, piano recitals, and soccer games.
- Make pizza together.
- Choose before grandchildren arrive what you

want to be called. Otherwise, one of the first nonsense syllables uttered in your presence may become your name.

- Don't iron underwear!

38 ❀ Encourage Just-Me-and-Mom Times

Someone said, "A son is a son until he takes a wife, but a daughter is a daughter all of her life."

While both extremes are extreme, there is some truth in that moms and daughters seem to be closer in adulthood than moms and sons. So another tip for being a great mother-in-law is to intentionally keep the relationship open with your son.

One friend who lives close to her son and daughter-in-law says her son jogs each morning and often stops by for a quick cup of coffee. Another friend of ours has a standing date with his eighty-year-old mother. Each Wednesday he takes her out to lunch.

My married sons live in other states—definitely not close enough for a jog or a weekly lunch—so some of our best communication happens over the phone.

Attitude: I will look for one-on-one time with my son or daughter without making his or her spouse feel excluded.

We're not talking about a big investment of time. Even fifteen to thirty minutes can help you stay connected. Sometimes, you can say things when you are alone with your son or daughter that you just can't say when you are all together. Maybe you can tag along on an errand, or perhaps you are the two early birds or the two night owls in the family. But don't abuse the privilege—that can be interpreted as possessiveness, and possessiveness doesn't build relationships.

Action: Ways to keep your relationship with your son or daughter healthy and growing

- Write a newsy letter and share what's going on in your life.
- Take him or her out to breakfast or brunch.
- Wing it. Look for times you find yourselves alone together and seize the moment.
- If there is a real problem, be willing to confront your son or daughter, but do it in private. Help him or her get help if needed. (For instance, if he or she has a drug dependency, talk in private and suggest a treatment program. Later he or she will thank you.)

39 Share Life's Struggles

It wasn't a planned conversation, but it is one I will long remember. On a recent visit to see my mother we discovered some intriguing family history. My brother was also present, and together we got Mother talking about her courtship with our dad. He used to travel over a hundred miles on dirt roads to spend several hours with her. That's real love!

But the best story she told was how for two years he asked her to marry him. Decision making wasn't Mother's strength. She wouldn't say yes or no until he told her he tore up the marriage license. Once she agreed to marry him, she found out that he still had the license. He was too stubborn and too frugal to destroy it!

Gene and I loved hearing the stories of our parents' courtship. But even more interesting were Mother's recollections of their first year of marriage —not easy by any standard.

They lived with my grandmother and aunt, and my brother arrived a few weeks before their first anniversary. My dad lost his job right after they got married. Things were tough, and as Mother shared with us, we found a new appreciation for who she is and what she has experienced. Transparency builds relationships. It's OK, even desirable, to be real with our in-laws.

Attitude: *I want to be a real person with my son- or daughter-in-law and foster a relationship in which we can share life's struggles.*

Another aspect of growing up in the South is that you naturally learn to speak "Southern Gush." It's a simple language. You simply say the polite thing whether you mean it or not—and usually you don't. It leads to hollow relationships, especially where in-laws are concerned.

How much better to be real and transparent. If you're doing something that totally irritates the other person (or vice versa), how much better to talk about it, find a compromise, and move on. Be willing to share your real self with your daughter- or son-in-law. The bad comes with the good. When you're willing to be open, then your in-law may be willing to be open with you.

Action: *Ways I can be real and transparent*

- Share your life experiences, both the good and the hard times.
- Be willing to admit it when you are wrong.
- Throw away your "perfect face."

- Resist the temptation to say things you don't mean.
- Write a short note to let your in-law know you identify with his or her hurts and disappointments.

40 ❀ Offer Alternatives

Our family has a ski history. As our boys were growing up we lived in Austria, and if you lived in Austria you skied. However, when we moved back to the States, skiing soon became something we did in the past. Then one winter our niece decided to get married in Colorado right before Christmas. Since we all planned to be at the wedding, we immediately heard opportunity knocking. Visions of family ski times together filled our imagination. We decided to rent a condo in the Colorado mountains for a family ski vacation. Simple? You've got to be kidding.

As we tried to plan our ski vacation, it immediately became confusing. It's not always easy to coordinate our own schedule, but coordinating three couples was ridiculous. Soon we felt we were back in the parenting role trying to direct this operation instead of providing a gift to our sons and daughters-in-law. We backed up and started all over again. This time we gave choices.

Attitude: *When trying to help my married children and their spouses, I will give choices, not ultimatums. I will be sensitive to their situation and feelings.*

Trying to coordinate our skiing vacation was a harder job than being a wedding coordinator for our niece's wedding. So we stepped back, reevaluated the situation and gave choices when we could.

First we looked at our schedule and determined the dates we could work with. Then we looked at our finances. Prices before Christmas vacation were definitely the best value so we picked the dates and location. We also found an area where you could ski free. Then we had the tourist agency send condo information to each couple. We all looked through the brochures and each person gave input. Together we picked one within our price range.

During the ski vacation, everyone chose when he or she wanted to ski, sleep, read, or whatever. No one pressured anyone to do anything. We let the younger generation cook, but we took turns cleaning up after the meals. For us it worked great.

Giving choices works at other times too. When we offer to take one couple out for dinner, we give them a few choices of restaurants within our budget. Once when we were visiting one son and daughter-in-law, we knew their finances were tight so we offered to either take them to Sam's Warehouse and spend what we would on a nice dinner out or go out for dinner. They chose the dinner, but it was their choice and we felt we were following their lead.

Offering choices helps us stay out of their business and finances and lets them make the final decision. Plus, it's great not to have to make all the decisions. It definitely facilitates a more adult relationship.

Action: Ways to give choices when appropriate

- Let them choose between eating out or staying in.
- Whenever appropriate, offer several different options. For instance, ask, "When we visit, we could plan to stay for two or three nights. What is best for you?"

41 ❧ Realize That You and Your Married Children Are Not in the Same Season of Life

"You're going where? We don't even want to hear about it!" was the response of one of our married sons as we told him about a possible trip to the Orient.

We've been in the empty nest for several years, and as Dave says, "This may be the best stage of family life." For sure it's a different season of life from the one our children are in. They are young professionals just getting started in their careers. Maybe your children are in the early parenting years. Whatever season of life your children are in, you are probably in a different one. Realizing this can help alleviate tension.

Attitude: I will seek to understand my son- or daughter-in-law's goals and try to understand life from his or her perspective.

To simply admit to each other that we are in different seasons of life is a starting place for better understanding. Nowhere does this manifest itself more than in family-owned businesses. The younger generation is ready to dig in, work hard, and invest in the future by expanding the company's base of business. The older generation's desire may be to wind down, take the profits, kick back, and enjoy life. You may not be involved in a family business, but you may find your goals are just as different. It helps to try to understand both sides—your situation and that of your son or daughter and their mates'.

A difference in perspective can also be apparent when grandchildren arrive. Recently I was asked about my three pregnancies, and honestly, I couldn't remember anything really negative or difficult. It takes some intentional empathy to identify and sympathize with a daughter-in-law who is experiencing morning sickness.

However, you only have to baby-sit for a couple of hours to remember how much energy it takes to keep up with a toddler. I love what Bill Cosby once said: "Give me a dozen two-year-olds and I'll conquer the world!" Perhaps your in-law is struggling to balance a job outside the home with parenting young children; stress and time pressure is just a way of life. Forget the phrase, "When I was your age . . ." When you were their age, this world was different!

Action: Ways to understand life from your in-law's perspective

- Intentionally look at life from his or her point of view.
- Don't complain about how hectic your life is. Believe me, it's all relative.
- Make a list of practical ways you can help.
- Research support groups that benefit them, such as MOM's Support Groups (for moms with all age children) and MOM's & DAD's Support Groups (specifically for parents of pre- and early adolescents).*
- When an in-law is changing careers, take an interest. Become educated about his or her new challenge.
- When someone is overwhelmed, do something big. Keep the kids for a week, or take your daughter-in-law on a fun trip.

* For information about these and other family enrichment resources write to: Marriage Alive, P.O. Box 90303, Knoxville, TN 37990.

42 ❀ Don't Discuss One Couple with Another

This is wise advice from my friend who has several married children, and I'm trying to follow it. She told me how during the first couple of years of having married kids, they all came to her with complaints about the other siblings and their spouses. Without realizing it, she became their dumping ground. They expected her to be the mediator. After all, she did like peace. It didn't work. Each time they got together, there were tears and misunderstandings.

Finally she declared her independence. Her new rule was, "Gripe at the person you are irritated with." She took down her mediation shingle and things greatly improved.

You may be able to avoid some bad times by adopting her rule sooner rather than later. Family relationships are complicated, and the more people we add to the inner circle, the more opportunities for misunderstandings. Remembering that is helping me to keep my mouth closed!

Attitude: *I will not discuss one couple with the other. Each is unique and different from the other. I choose not to compare one with the other.*

It's not always easy to stay neutral, but it's worth striving for. It will definitely cut down on misunderstandings. I find when I concentrate on each person's uniqueness and positive qualities, I just don't have as great a need to air my feelings.

Action: Ways to avoid comparing one couple with another

- Resist comparing finances, housing, parenting techniques, life-styles, or the way they dress.
- Remember, "Comparison is the root of all agony!"
- Don't be a carrier pigeon for messages from other family members.

43 ✿ Remember That Whatever Happens You Are Still a Mother-in-Law

Hopefully, this is one tip you will not need, but Nancy's mother-in-law did. Here is Nancy's story. "My mother died during the first year of my marriage. It was a very difficult time, and my mother-in-law was incredible. We became very close and were almost like mother and daughter. We argued with each other. We were real. She was very supportive but never said, 'This is what you need to do.'

"Fast forward four years and two babies. Our second child was born with serious problems. My husband had a hard time with the whole situation and our marriage began to fall apart. One day he simply left, and I was devastated. Thank goodness, my mother-in-law stood by me. I don't know what I would have done without her."

Attitude: Whatever happens to this marriage, I will remain supportive and try to stay in touch with my son- or daughter-in-law.

When Nancy's marriage fell apart, her mother-in-law remained supportive and helpful. Nancy needed to go to work to support her family. In no way did Nancy's closet resemble a working woman's wardrobe, so her mother-in-law took her shopping and bought her an attractive business outfit. She stood by Nancy through the terminal illness of her two-year-old daughter. And in the months afterwards she was thoughtful in so many ways, once sending flowers with a note saying, "I know how you feel. I miss her too."

In a similar situation, could you be as supportive? Admittedly, the end of a marriage is a difficult situation, and you will have to be sensitive to your own son or daughter. You will need to respect his or her wishes as well. Strive to find the balance.

Another mother-in-law's son was killed tragically in a car accident. In spite of her own suffering, she went out and bought an expensive jacket that she knew her son was going to buy for his wife's birthday. She sent it to her daughter-in-law with a card saying, "This is something Bob would have wanted you to have."

Action: Ways to stay in touch and be supportive

- Remember birthdays and other special days.
- When things are tough, be supportive in practical ways. Give financial aid, buy groceries, or help pay the phone and electric bill. Whatever it is that you can do to help, do it.
- Give little gifts of love. It's especially nice to

give something frivolous like perfume or a box of favorite chocolates or tickets to a movie.
• Volunteer some of your time to help with grandchildren or other needs.

44 ❖ Think Ahead, Plan Ahead

There is life after in-laws and grandchildren. However, it's a life that may require more planning. I use to think about how simple life would be when our children grew up, got married, and left home. This stage of life definitely has its merits, but simplicity is not one of them.

Each marriage joins together at least two more families. With so many blended families today, it's even more complicated. The family circle just gets bigger and bigger. There's more family to love, but also more opportunities to misunderstand each other.

Attitude: I will think ahead and plan ahead. I will remain in control of my own life and not base what I do or don't do on others.

Thinking and planning ahead can help to chart the course and avoid shipwrecked relationships. As family life gets complicated, it's easy to feel out of control, but with a little prethinking and preplanning you can keep healthy relationships afloat. Now is the time to come up with your own strategy. When your son or daughter and his or her mate come to visit, how much adapting are you willing to do? What is your grandchildren policy? Which family traditions are flexible? One Christmas we adapted so much we almost missed Christmas. The next year we planned what we would do and we did it. Participation by sons and daughters-in-law was totally up to them, and it worked out well. We're learning not to base our plans on theirs.

When we totally defer to our married children and their spouses and kids, we put a terrible burden on them. Remember you have a life of your own—or should have! No one wants to feel responsible for someone else's happiness. Vacations together may be great but certainly not every vacation. Keeping grandchildren may be fun, but the how, when, where, and how long should be your decision. Your in-laws and children will respect you much more if you're clear about how much you want to be involved. So once you've made your plans, communicate them. It'll help you have smoother sailing in the future. And remember, nothing has to be set in concrete. Tomorrow's situation may be different from today's. You've earned the right to change your mind.

Action: Ways to think and plan ahead

- Make a list of what you're not going to do. For instance, decide now whether or not a month is too long for grandchildren to visit.
- Before a family get-together on a major holiday, let your plans be known. Say, "We're plan-

ning to go to the midnight service. You can go with us if you like."

- Plan a vacation without the extended family.
- Think through your family traditions. Which ones are the really important ones? Which ones can be more flexible?

45 ❀ Give Encouragement

I love encouragement. So if I'm working on a new book, I send the manuscript to Lillian. I can count on her to compliment my writing as she pores through each manuscript. My editor critiques my writing, complete with red marks and notes to rewrite, but not Lillian.

Everyone has some positive qualities. It's your assignment as the mother-in-law to find them. Maybe, for you, looking for the positive with your in-law is easy. You liked and admired him or her from the first day you met.

If this describes you, great; if not, you have a choice. You are the key player, and your attitude can make the difference.

Attitude: *I choose to focus on the positive and look for ways to give encouragement.*

Do you see the glass half empty or half full? Do you look at your son- or daughter-in-law as half incredible or half terrible? No one is perfect. Daily, you have the opportunity to choose to concentrate on the positive or the negative.

Appreciate the maturity you observe, ignore the immaturity. Look at your son- or daughter-in-law as a sort of hidden treasure. He or she has many positive attributes, and it's up to you to discover them.

Maybe your son- or daughter-in-law is going through a hard time and simply needs a break. What can you do to offer encouragement? Maybe you could give a morning or an afternoon to take care of the children so your in-law could have some time alone. Or maybe you could send a little gift or a card to lift his or her spirits. Once when I was looking for a way to give just a little extra encouragement to one of my daughters-in-law, I found a lovely pewter cream and pitcher set on sale that I thought she would like. Hopefully as she uses it, it will be a pleasant reminder of my love for her.

Action: Ways to give encouragement

- Send a care package. Include a few surprises to show you've been observing the couple's changing taste as adults by including their favorite gourmet tea, coffee, or mustard in an attractive basket. Everyone loves an appropriate surprise.
- Avoid critical comments.
- Give your son- or daughter-in-law a chance to do something he or she has been wanting to do. Once Dave's mother took us to the ballet when we were living in Vienna. That was my desire, not Dave's.

- Give your in-law a book by a favorite author. Cookbooks make great gifts too.
- Give the couple a directory of bed & breakfast inns in their area, and tuck in a coupon for a twenty-four-hour getaway.

46 ❋ Put More Thought Than Money into Holiday Giving

Making new in-laws feel included and comfortable during the holiday season can be a real challenge, especially if finances are limited. Show me a newly married couple and chances are I can show you a couple whose cash flow is tight. What can you do to help relieve stress and create family harmony during the holiday season?

One Arp tradition I married into is that all the women in the family draw names. This keeps gift giving under control, and each person gets one nice gift. Our daughters-in-law have joined this Arp tradition. It's one way for them to get to know new relatives and feel part of the Arp clan.

Attitude: *I will look for ways to relieve the stress of holiday gift-giving.*

"What should I give my in-laws?" is not always an easy question to answer. It's good to set a dollar limit —the lower the better. As one of my sons said, "Our presents have a lot of thought behind them but not so much money."

You've known your own children long enough to

know what they like and dislike, but you have no such history with your in-laws. Here are some gift suggestions we've collected over the years.

For the male member of the family, we suggest sweat pants and shirts, athletic equipment and clothes, or gifts that go with his hobbies. Avoid giving ties, and don't give gifts in an effort to change his style.

For the female member of the family, try perfume, particularly if she has a favorite scent; earrings, if you are familiar with her style; or athletic equipment and clothes. You might also look through catalogs together and note what she likes.

You could give a gift to the couple. Consider giving them both food (a honey baked ham, frozen steaks, a gourmet food basket), house plants, compact discs or cassettes, a coupon for a dinner out, a piece of crystal or china, or a magazine subscription. These are all things that they can enjoy together.

Action: Ways to make holiday gift-giving enjoyable with in-laws

- Set a dollar limit on gifts.
- Draw names and give one nice gift.
- Exchange wish lists with each other.
- Save receipts for returns.

47 ❀ Find the Comfort Zone between Intimacy and Distance

When I asked "What is your best advice for one who wants to be a great mother-in-law?" I received the same answer in four different countries. Two simple words; "Stay Away!" This was not the answer I was looking for, but it gave me a clue to one big problem area in in-law relationships. How do you find the comfort zone between intimacy and distance?

Picture a seesaw with intimacy on one end and distance on the other. What you want to do is find the appropriate balance in your relationship. Those who say, "stay away" probably never found that balance. It is a continual balancing act, and often I'm off balance. Also, the many changes in life create the need to adjust that balance.

Susan, a new mom, told me about how she felt when she was in the hospital when her first child was born. She loved all the attention she received during her pregnancy. Then the baby arrived. It was great fun when all the family came to the hospital to visit her and to see the baby, but then they all said "good-bye" and went out to eat together. She was left alone

in her hospital room with her new baby while everyone else was celebrating at her favorite restaurant!
She felt more distance at this point than she wanted
to feel. Then, in the following weeks both her mother
and mother-in-law were continually around to give a
helping hand. Their motives were great, but at this
point Susan just wanted a little space. It's hard to find
the balance.

Attitude: *I will strive to find the appropriate*
balance between being too involved and not
involved enough.

We want to be involved with our adult married children, but we have to work together at finding the
balance. Some families enjoy getting together each
Sunday for dinner while others say, "Isn't it great, we
get to see our married kids several times a year!"

There are so many factors: where you live, children, jobs, financial resources. This is one area
where you must find what works for you. When you
are together, don't let your expectations get inflated.
The more in-laws you add, the more complicated relationships become. You can't be as intimate with everyone as you were with your nuclear family.

Action: *Ways to find the comfort zone*

- Think about the past. Is your mother-in-law
  style to hover or to ignore or somewhere in
  between?
- Talk it out with your adult children and their
  spouses. What does it take to make each per-

son feel comfortable? One family asked each couple this question. One daughter-in-law said, "I need to feel included." Another said, "I need some time alone away from people."

• Discuss holidays beforehand and have a game plan.

48 ❀ Remember Birthdays and Other Special Occasions

Lillian is the kind of mother-in-law you want to honor, so when Lillian and David's fiftieth wedding anniversary was approaching, we planned, along with Dave's sister, a luncheon at a lovely restaurant in a Chicago suburb. The luncheon was the day after one of our sons got married, which may help excuse the following mix-up.

When Dave's sister, Ginia, arrived at the restaurant, Dave was all set with the video camera to record their parents' grand entrance. What he videotaped was the shocked look on his sister's face when Ginia realized we were expecting her to bring the anniversary couple! Where were their parents? They were at the hotel twenty minutes away waiting for someone to pick them up. Hurrying to the hotel to retrieve them, we tried a shortcut and got lost. We arrived back at the restaurant with the honorees two hours late! Fortunately, both Lillian and David, Sr. have a great sense of humor and still laugh about their fiftieth wedding anniversary celebration and how their children forgot them.

The moral of this story? Just in case your daughter- or son-in-law is not so well-endowed with a sense of humor, try to remember special days and days that desperately need to be special.

My friend Laura is great at remembering special days. Recently when her daughter-in-law was visiting to apply for a new job, Laura took her shopping for a business suit. It wasn't her birthday and it was not expected. It was just something Laura wanted to do to encourage her daughter-in-law.

Attitude: I will be thoughtful and loving to my son- or daughter-in-law by remembering birthdays and other occasions.

What can you do today to remember your in-law? How can you reach a balance? Too many gifts can be perceived as manipulation, too few as not caring. We try to be unpredictable and set no patterns. Remembrances can be simple—a letter expressing your joy in having them as part of your family, a small check suggesting a "dessert out" date, a coupon to baby-sit. Think back to your early marriage years. What did your mother-in-law do for you—or what do you wish she had done?

A word to the wise: Know why you are being thoughtful. Everyone loves gratitude, but if your motive is to be appreciated, you may be setting yourself up for major disappointment.

However, gratitude may come when you don't expect it. One year we spent Christmas with Dave's sister and her family. All our family had been there earlier, but couldn't stay for Christmas, so we celebrated our own Christmas early. Presents were thoughtfully exchanged. Imagine my surprise when on Christmas Day an extra present appeared under the tree. Its tag read, "This is for a wonderful mother from your son and daughter-in-law who appreciate you." We looked around the room. I was the only one with daughters-in-law so we assumed the present was for me. I remember thinking, "Those kids should not have done this! They already gave me wonderful presents. They can't afford this." I was right. They couldn't afford it! It wasn't for me at all. Ginia's brother-in-law had left his present for his mother under the wrong tree. We skillfully rewrapped the present and passed it on to the appropriate mother-in-law.

Action: Ways to remember my son- or daughter-in-law on special occasions

- Send notes and cards. All crisp, green enclosures are appreciated!
- Choose gifts thoughtfully. They may require more time than money.
- Remember why you're giving.
- Be unpredictable.
- Give gifts without creating obligation on their part or on yours.

49 ❀ Don't Compete

"My mother-in-law is the wicked witch of the west," said one young mom. "If my husband sides with me, she gets angry and tries to make him feel guilty. If I say something is black, she calls it white. And then she compares me with her daughter who is my age and, by the way, is perfect!"

A wise person said that comparison is the root of all agony, and he was right. There's no place for comparing or competing in mother-in-law relationships. The temptation is to compare in-laws with your own kids and in-laws with other in-laws. The best advice I can give is "don't!"

Attitude: *I will acknowledge I am not competing for my son's or daughter's love and realize there's enough love to go around.*

It's great not to be compared with Dave's sister (who is the only super mom I know, is multi-talented, and wears a size five). Lillian simply includes me in the family. I have never felt a spirit of competition.

One great joy in life is to see your son or daughter happily married and totally dedicated to his or her spouse. Your job as the mother-in-law is to respect each new in-law that joins your family. Competition is outlawed. There's enough love to go around. Respect each relationship and realize that each is different and unique.

Remember that as the relationship between your offspring and his or her spouse deepens, they'll spend more and more time with each other. Their first priority is their marital relationship. As mother and mother-in-law, respect that relationship and don't compete for attention.

Action: Ways to avoid competition

- See your in-law as an individual. Each relationship is unique.
- Accept visits and time spent with you as a gift, not your right.
- Treat your daughter- or son-in-law as you would like to be treated.
- Never put your offspring in the position of having to choose allegiance between you and his or her mate.

50 ❋ Take a Mother-in-Law Pill Every Morning

What I need is a mother-in-law pill. One that includes a daily dose of love, acceptance, patience, and tolerance would be great.

The problem with becoming a mother-in-law is that it often happens about the same time we begin going through menopause. While this may not be the easiest transition in life, there are some things we can do to maintain our sanity and healthy in-law relationships.

We're not just getting older, we're getting better. This can be a time of new horizons if we focus on the future instead of the past. "Wait a minute" said my friend, Marge. "I just can't agree with you. What's 'better' about hot flashes and sleepless nights! I'm not sure I like this stage of life."

To be honest, few of us would choose menopause, but we can choose to manage it appropriately. It's up to us to take control of this stage of life and do what we need to do to maintain our sanity and equilibrium. We can choose our attitude.

***Attitude:** I choose to look at this time of life as a new beginning—as my second adulthood, and I will do what I can to maintain a healthy*

body, a proper mental perspective, and a positive relationship with my son- or daughter-in-law and other family members.

First, educate yourself about this new passage of life. The best book I've read on the subject is *The Silent Passage* by Gail Sheehy. She brings up many issues and decisions that only you can make. Sheehy discusses the pros and cons of hormone replacement therapy and gives the reader enough understanding and knowledge to ask her doctor intelligent and relevant questions.

Second, get a complete physical and do what you can do to live a healthy life style. I'm a great believer in exercise, and I can tell a real difference on the days I miss it. If there is ever a time to evaluate your eating habits, this is it. Whatever you do to feel better about yourself will flow over into your family relationships.

Third, remember that this too shall pass. It's not the end of the world or the end of your life. You are simply moving on to a new era.

Action: Ways to maintain a healthy body and mental perspective during menopause

- Eat sensibly. Begin to count grams of fat and watch your cholesterol.
- Consider joining an aerobics class or working out at a gym.
- Make an intelligent choice about hormone replacement. Ask your doctor about anything that concerns you. Don't be shy.

- Read *The Silent Passage* and other books on the subject.
- Be open with your family as to how you feel and where you are in life.

51 ❧ Tolerate Small Irritations

It's wonderful to feel comfortable with another person and especially wonderful when that other person is your mother-in-law. Lillian always seemed to sense that our friendship was a long-term one. Over the years she has invested in our relationship by not sweating the small stuff. I hope that after I've been a mother-in-law for thirty years the same thing can be said of me. In the meantime, how can we deal with small irritations—the nickel and dime annoyances we all experience?

Some things aren't worth getting upset about, especially when we acknowledge that it's the relationship that is most important. Whatever the irritation is, it will probably soon be forgotten. When you get irritated, ask yourself "What difference will it make in twenty-five years?"

Attitude: I will acknowledge that this is a long-term relationship. I choose to tolerate small irritations and realize that they are present in all relationships.

Look at it from another perspective. From time to time you probably also irritate your son- or daughter-in-law. Sometimes it's best to not take life so seriously. Do whatever you can to foster fun, to loosen up and laugh. As one mother-in-law of forty years put it, "I make mistakes too. Their mistakes are just different from mine. I've learned to overlook a lot and to accept that they just do things differently from me. Different doesn't mean wrong."

Action: Ways to tolerate small irritations

- Process frustrations through physical activities like gardening or polishing the silver or brass.
- Take a deep breath.
- Take a bubble bath.
- Take a walk.
- Take a break! Go to the library or to a park or to a small café for a cup of tea.

52 ✦ Choose to Be a Great Mother-in-Law

"What's your best advice for getting along with in-laws?" is a question I have asked many people, and I have gotten so many different answers, many of which made it into these pages. But one suggestion I saved for last. Our friend Larry said, "Simply select a great mother-in-law!"

While life doesn't work that way, there is wisdom in his answer if you change a couple of words and make it, "Choose to be a great mother-in-law." It takes two to build a healthy in-law relationship, but it can begin with you. By the way, I've met Larry's mother-in-law, and he did select a great one!

I've never met a mother whose goal was to be a bad mother-in-law. Talking with a young friend whose mother-in-law drives her crazy, I commented, "I hope I will never be like that!"

Her response? "You won't be if you're already thinking about it and monitoring yourself now."

That you're interested enough to read this book indicates you're on the right track. It may help to remember that you're not the keeper of your daughter- or son-in-law. As a parent you tried to nurture, to protect, to motivate, and to be an agent of change.

Not so with an in-law. You don't want to interfere. You simply want to be a great mother-in-law!

Attitude: I will take the initiative to think about and monitor my actions as a mother-in-law.

Here is where suggestions end and life begins. You now have 52 ways to be a great mother-in-law. Not all of them will apply to your situation, but some will. Consider the ones that do. Remember that relationships are fluid and are ever changing. You have the opportunity to change your in-law relationships for the better. By thinking about your role as a mother-in-law and monitoring yourself, you can be a great mother-in-law. The choice is yours!

Action: Ways to be a great mother-in-law

- Bless, don't bless out!
- Be a peer and friend.
- Be balanced. Avoid extremes.
- Be yourself.
- Pray daily for contentment. Here is a meditation I've often used:

Teach me how to find contentment as I grow older.
Teach me how to be a person others want to be
around, not avoid.
Teach me how to enjoy the gift of life,
to enjoy each day, to have no self-pity.
Teach me how to treasure memories
and plan for tomorrow with enthusiasm.

*May I be thankful for the times we as a family
go our separate ways.
May I be thankful for the special times
we feel like a family again.
May I be thankful for the privilege of being both a
mother and a mother-in-law!*

Claudia Arp is the mother of three adult sons and has two daughters-in-law.

With her husband, Dave, Claudia founded and now directs Marriage Alive International, a marriage and family enrichment organization. Their Marriage Alive Workshop is popular across the United States and in Europe.

Claudia is the founder of the MOM's Support Groups, a family enrichment resource program with groups throughout the United States and in Europe and Asia. She is also the author of *Beating the Winter Blues, Sanity in the Summertime,* and *The Marriage Track*. Claudia has a B.S. in Home Economics Education from University of Georgia.